MONSTER HUNTERS
FINDING
DRAGONS
By Therese Shea
Gareth Stevens
PUBLISHING

Please visit our website, www.garethstevens.com. For a free color catalog of all our high-quality books, call toll free 1-800-542-2595 or fax 1-877-542-2596.

Library of Congress Cataloging-in-Publication Data
Names: Shea, Therese, author.
Title: Finding dragons / Therese Shea.
Description: Buffalo, New York : Gareth Stevens Publishing, [2026] | Series: Monster hunters | Includes index.
Identifiers: LCCN 2024049201 (print) | LCCN 2024049202 (ebook) | ISBN 9781482472080 (library binding) | ISBN 9781482472073 (paperback) | ISBN 9781482472097 (ebook)
Subjects: LCSH: Dragons–Juvenile literature. | Dragons–Folklore–Juvenile literature. | Map reading–Juvenile literature. | Geography–Juvenile literature.
Classification: LCC GR830.D7 S38 2026 (print) | LCC GR830.D7 (ebook) | DDC 398.24/54–dc23/eng/20241206
LC record available at https://lccn.loc.gov/2024049201
LC ebook record available at https://lccn.loc.gov/2024049202

Published in 2026 by
Gareth Stevens Publishing
2544 Clinton Street
Buffalo, NY 14224

Designer: Andrea Davison-Bartolotta
Editor: Therese Shea

Photo credits: Cover, pp. 1 (dragon), 14, 20 Shutterstock AI/Shutterstock.com; cover, p. 1, series art (glowing compass rose) LoveDesignShop/Shutterstock.com; series art (cardinal compass rose) Angela Ksen/Shutterstock.com; series art (ordinal compass rose) jame05/Shutterstock.com; series art (fact box rope border) LanaN/Shutterstock.com; series art (fact box wood) EE SPACE/Shutterstock.com; series art (map background) Olha Andreichyn/Shutterstock.com; series art (curled paper background) MIGUEL G. SAAVEDRA/Shutterstock.com; series art (flat paper) Paladin12/Shutterstock.com; p. 5 (chart background) Muhammad Mandalaaa/Shutterstock.com; p. 5 (main) Eli Unger/Shutterstock.com; p. 7 Kumeko/Shutterstock.com; pp. 9 (map), 23 (map) PorcupenWorks/Shutterstock.com; p. 9 (main) ABCDstock/Shutterstock.com; pp. 11, 13 (map) pingebat/Shutterstock.com; p. 11 (main) The South Wind/Shutterstock.com; p. 12 SouthernCrx/Shutterstock.com; pp. 15 (dragon), 19 (dragon) Vac1/Shutterstock.com; p. 15 (map) PorcupenWorks/Shutterstock.com; p. 17 (flag) iunewind/Shutterstock.com; p. 17 (main) Microscope/Shutterstock.com; p. 19 (map) WHISKHEELS/Shutterstock.com; p. 20 AuraArt/Shutterstock.com; p. 21 (inset) Fokografie/Shutterstock.com; p. 21 (main) aaron choi/Shutterstock.com; p. 23 (main) Dmitry Tonkonog and Ksenia Fedosova/File:20130816 Drachenfels.jpg/Wikimedia Commons; pp. 24-25 Art_rich/Shutterstock.com; p. 27 David Pimborough/Shutterstock.com; pp. 28, 29 (map) Janos Levente/Shutterstock.com; pp. 28, 29 (paper) AKaiser/Shutterstock.com.

Printed in the United States of America

CPSIA compliance information: Batch #CSGS26: For further information contact Gareth Stevens at 1-800-542-2595.

Find us on

CONTENTS

Words in the glossary appear in **bold** type the first time they are used in the text.

DRAGON HUNT!

Myths aren't just stories. They tell us about gods, heroes, events, and creatures that people once believed to be true. Some still believe.

Many **cultures** around the world have myths about dragons. Some tales are hundreds or even thousands of years old. Do they have some truth?

In this book, you'll travel the world looking for dragons. You'll go to the source of several myths and hope for a dragon sighting! Don't forget to pack your maps—and your map skills—to find the way.

Sometimes you don't have to go too far to see a dragon. Cultural **celebrations** in some cities may include a dragon puppet.

Even within one culture's myths, dragons can look and act differently. Here are some common features.

DRAGON FEATURES

- appear like lizards or snakes but larger
- may breathe fire or poisonous breath
- may have more than one head
- may have no legs, two legs, or four legs
- may be good or evil
- represent, or stand for, power

NOW ENTERING ASIA

Earth has seven large landmasses called continents: Asia, Africa, North America, South America, Antarctica, Europe, and Australia. To start the search for a dragon, you'll first go to Asia. It's the largest continent. Asia is also the most populated continent. That means it's the continent with the most people.

It won't be hard to find stories of dragons in Asia. Many different Asian cultures have special tales about these creatures. Some of these stories are connected to certain locations, or places.

You can see on this map that Asia is the largest of the seven continents. The smallest is Australia.

Behind the Myth

Some old maps included drawings of dragons. That sometimes meant the mapmaker didn't know much about the area.

UNDER BEIJING

You'll start looking in Beijing, China. Beijing is the capital of China. In Chinese myths, dragons control water. They're snakelike but may be able to change shape.

In one tale, a large dragon lived in Beijing. He grew angry when people began to move and build there. The dragon planned to flood the city. A hero named Yao Guangxiao and a general named Yue Fei fought the dragon and the dragon's son. They trapped the dragons beneath the city, where they still are said to live.

The Yue Fei Temple is said to guard the well where one dragon is trapped.

Behind the Myth

Beijing is located in a low, flat area near several rivers. The city once had a problem with flooding.

A compass rose is a map **symbol** that tells you directions. Use the one here to find Beijing in the northern part of China.

A VISIT TO VIETNAM

Next, go south. Trace a path from China to Vietnam on the map. In Vietnamese myths, dragons are signs of power and good luck.

In the year 1010, King Le Thai To established a new capital city on the Red River. As he arrived there by boat, he saw a golden dragon soaring, or rising, into the sky. This was a good omen, or sign. The king called the city Thang Long, which means "Soaring Dragon." Today, it's called Hanoi. It's still the capital of Vietnam.

BEHIND THE MYTH

Later Vietnamese rulers claimed to have seen golden dragons too. Dragons became a symbol of royal authority.

This compass rose shows the four main compass directions: north, south, east, and west. These are called the cardinal directions.

These statues are on Ho Tay (West Lake) in Hanoi, Vietnam.

JUMPING UP TO JAPAN

Next, let's **investigate** a Japanese myth. Look at the map. To reach Japan, you'll travel northeast from Vietnam. Some myths say a dragon lives within the Japanese mountain called Fuji.

BEHIND THE MYTH

Many myths help explain nature and natural events. Long ago, the Japanese blamed dragons for **earthquakes** and **volcanoes**.

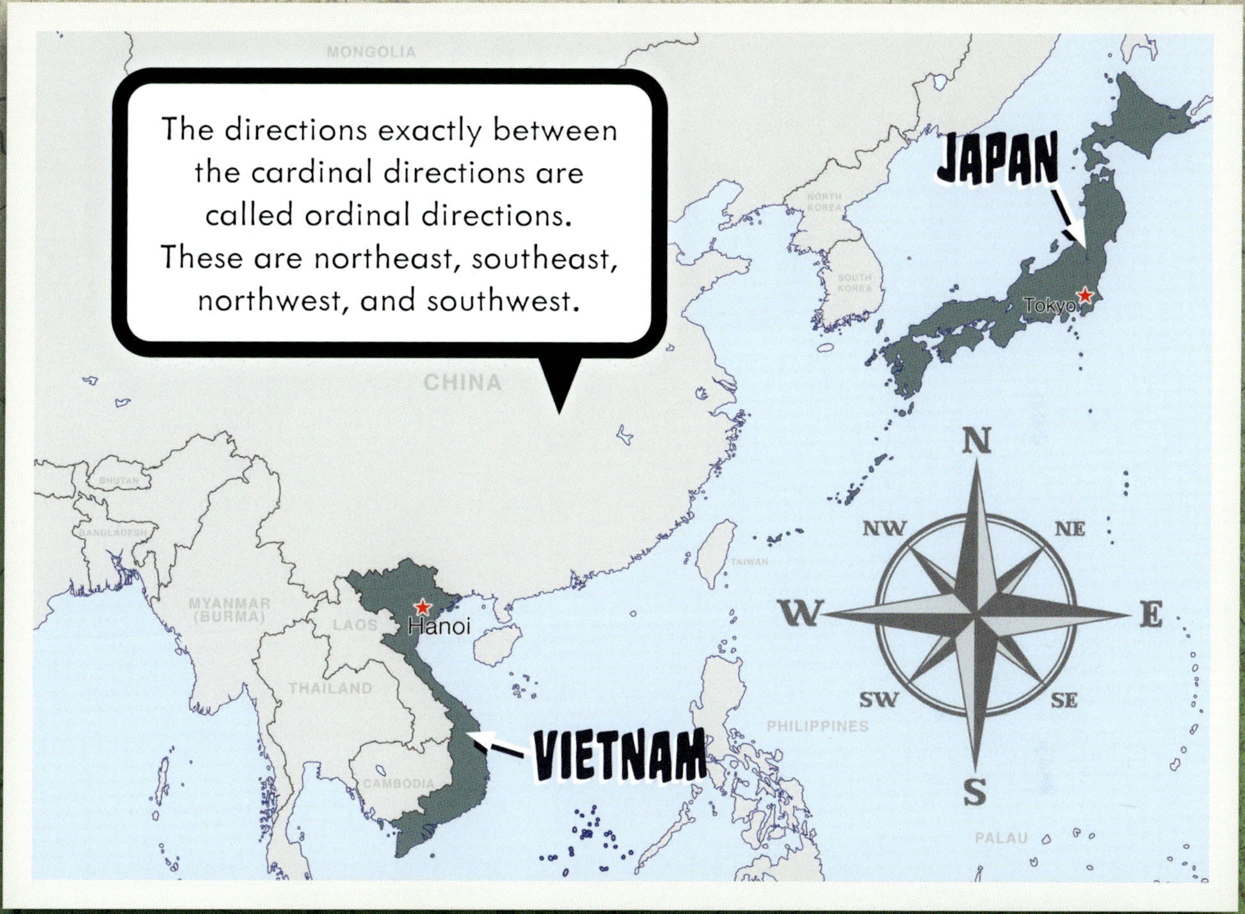

Mount Fuji is on the island of Honshu. It's the tallest mountain in Japan at 12,388 feet (3,776 m) tall. It's also a volcano! It last erupted in 1707. Today, hundreds of thousands of people climb Mount Fuji in the summer. The rest of the year, its top is covered with snow.

HEADING TOWARD EUROPE

Head west to learn about some dragon myths of Europe. In most European tales, dragons were evil creatures with wings and long tails. Some lived in caves. They often were said to be able to breathe fire. And they ate people!

The tale of Saint George and the dragon is one of the most famous dragon tales of Europe. The story comes from the country of Georgia. Georgia is located where the continents of Asia and Europe meet.

Georgia is south of Russia and east of the Black Sea. Use the compass rose to check these directions.

SAINT GEORGE AND THE DRAGON

Saint George was likely a real man who was a Roman soldier around 300 CE. He may have been killed by the Roman ruler Diocletian because he was a **Christian**. After his death, George was named a Christian saint.

Tales began to be told about George's deeds after his death. Hundreds of years after, a tale from Georgia told of how George saved a princess from a dragon. After he killed the dragon, he received riches from the princess's father. George gave his treasure to the poor.

Tbilisi is the capital of the country of Georgia. Visitors to this city can see a golden monument of Saint George killing the dragon.

Behind the Myth

The largest red cross on the Georgia flag represents Saint George.

MOUNTAINOUS COUNTRY

Switzerland is your next stop. It's west of Georgia, in Europe. Switzerland is a landlocked country. That means it's surrounded by other countries. It doesn't touch a sea or an ocean. Switzerland is a mountainous country, which means it has many mountains.

A Swiss dragon myth has to do with Mount Pilatus. Mount Pilatus is located in the center of the country, near Lake Lucerne. It rises about 6,983 feet (2,128 m) at its highest point. It's a mountain massif, which means it has several peaks, or pointed tops.

The coloring on some maps shows areas with higher **elevations.** The brownish areas here tell us where mountains are in Switzerland. The Jura Mountains are in the northwest and the Alps are in the south and east.

Dragons were said to live in and around Mount Pilatus. According to one story, a dragon crashed near a field at the bottom of the mountain. A farmer found a stone the dragon left. It could heal people!

Another tale tells of how a Swiss hero named Arnold von Winkelried killed a dragon. Arnold was killed himself when a drop of dragon blood froze the blood in his body.

Still another tale tells of a storm washing a dragon down the mountain. It fell into the Reuss River.

Mount Pilatus has **inspired** many dragon myths over the years. Some still call it the Mountain of Dragons. Today, you can take a cable car to the top!

FAFNIR THE FEARFUL DRAGON

Travel north from Switzerland, and you'll arrive in Germany. The countries share a border. Ancient Germanic people told tales of dragons too.

In one myth, a prince named Fafnir killed his father for a cursed treasure. Fafnir changed himself into a dragon so he could guard his riches. A hero named Siegfried later killed him. According to some tales, Fafnir had hidden his treasure in a cave in the hill called Drachenfels (Dragon's Rock). This is a real place in western Germany, on the Rhine River.

Behind the Myth

Some myths teach values. The story of Fafnir warns people not to be greedy or bad things may happen to them.

You can visit Drachenfels in Königswinter, Germany.

Volcanic activity formed Drachenfels long ago. An old castle lies on top today.

DRAGON ORIGINS?

It's time to go home. Which direction will you go? When you get there, think about the places you've been. Many are very, very far apart. Some think different cultures came up with dragon tales around the same time. How could that be?

Ancient peoples may have gotten the idea for dragons from dinosaur **fossils** they found. Whale bones on beaches could have inspired dragon myths too. So could smaller dragon-like creatures such as crocodiles and lizards.

Fossils like this look like they were from a creature of myth! Now we know they're from dinosaurs.

NEWER DRAGONS

Some dragon tales aren't as old as the ones you've just read about. English author J. R. R. Tolkien wrote about a dragon named Smaug in his 1937 book *The Hobbit*.

The 2021 Disney movie *Raya and the Last Dragon* is set in a land like Southeast Asia. It's not based on one myth but uses pieces from many tales. The story tells of a world in which humans and dragons live together.

Dragons appear in the Percy Jackson book series too. These stories are about Greek gods in today's world.

J. R. R. Tolkien knew a lot about myths. He used ideas from them when he wrote *The Hobbit*. Smaug is a bit like Fafnir, for example.

Behind the Myth

The Hobbit is about a small person-like creature who goes on an adventure to find a dragon's treasure.

DRAGONS SPOTTED!

These are just some of the many dragon myths around the world.
Beijing, China—The Yue Fei Temple is said to guard a well where a dragon is trapped.
Mount Fuji, Japan—Does a dragon live within Mount Fuji?
Hanoi, Vietnam—A ruler saw a golden dragon, a good omen for the capital city.
N
W
E
S

GLOSSARY

celebration: A time to show happiness for an event through activities such as eating or playing music.

Christian: A follower of Jesus Christ.

culture: The beliefs and ways of life of a group of people.

earthquake: A shaking of the ground caused by the movement of Earth's crust.

elevation: Height above sea level.

fossil: The marks or remains of plants and animals that formed over thousands or millions of years.

inspire: To cause someone to want to do something.

investigate: To search for clues about something.

symbol: A picture, shape, or object that stands for something else.

volcano: An opening in a planet's surface through which hot, liquid rock sometimes erupts, or flows out.

FOR MORE INFORMATION

Books

Loh-Hagan, Virginia. *Discover Dragons*. Ann Arbor, MI: Cherry Lake Publishing, 2023.

Novak, Sara. *The Genius Kid's Guide to Mythical Creatures*. Mendota Heights, MN: North Star Kids, 2023.

Websites

Dragon
kids.britannica.com/kids/article/dragon/353064
Check out interesting facts about these mythical beasts.

Natural History of Dragon
www.amnh.org/exhibitions/mythic-creatures/dragons/natural-history-of-dragons
Read more about what people have said about dragons throughout history.

Publisher's note to educators and parents: Our editors have carefully reviewed these websites to ensure that they are suitable for students. Many websites change frequently, however, and we cannot guarantee that a site's future contents will continue to meet our high standards of quality and educational value. Be advised that students should be closely supervised whenever they access the internet.

INDEX